Barbie Millicent Roberts

AN ORIGINAL

PHOTOGRAPHS BY

DAVID LEVINTHAL

PREFACE BY VALERIE STEELE

DOLLS STYLED BY LAURA MEISNER

A CONSTANCE SULLIVAN BOOK

PANTHEON BOOKS • NEW YORK • 1998

This book was planned, prepared, and produced by
Hummingbird Books Inc.

Library of Congress Cataloging-in-Publication Data
Levinthal, David.
Barbie Millicent Roberts / photographs by David Levinthal / preface by Valerie
Steele / dolls styled by Laura Meisner.
p. cm.
ISBN 0-375-40425-2
1. Fashion photography—Exhibitions. 2. Barbie dolls—Pictorial works—
Exhibitions. 3. Barbie dolls—Social aspects—Exhibitions. 4. Levinthal,
David—Exhibitions. II. Title.
TR679.L48   1998   668.7'221—dc21   98-6828   CIP

Random House Web Address: www.randomhouse.com

Printed in Italy

First Edition

Page 1: "Campus Sweetheart" (1965), a strapless bouffant evening gown
of white satin overlaid with panels of pink and red tulle.

Frontispiece: #2 Barbie, 1959. "Solo in the Spotlight" (1960–64).
This "mermaid" gown of spandex knit encrusted with Mylar
is a signature Barbie garment.

Facing page: Platinum blonde side-parted Bubble Cut Barbie, 1966.

#2 Barbie, 1959. "Easter Parade" (1959), a sleeveless cotton
print sheath worn with a black artist's-smock coat and silk organza bow hat,
is one of the most coveted Barbie costumes.

Barbie Millicent Roberts

AN ORIGINAL

Barbie was born during the golden age of the French haute couture, when girls everywhere dreamed of wearing the latest fashions from Paris. Barbie's miniature wardrobe brought such dreams closer to reality.

After World War II, Paris once again became the international capital of fashion. Wartime restrictions on fabric and decoration gave way to Christian Dior's "New Look" of 1947, which transformed the appearance of women's fashion. Other influential couturiers included Coco Chanel, Cristóbal Balenciaga, Jacques Fath, and Hubert de Givenchy. The structure of the couture had also been transformed—from the atelier to the global corporate conglomerate. Modern couturiers designed for a much larger clientele, licensing their creations to department stores and ready-to-wear manufacturers. Line-for-line copies of couture dresses were available at a fraction of the cost of the originals.

As a result, popular interest in fashion exploded. Movies such as *Funny Face* featured Audrey Hepburn flying to Paris to become a top fashion model. Even children's books such as *Eloise in Paris* showed girls in couture clothes.

In 1959, a new doll was launched by Mattel at the New York Toy Fair. Described as a "Teenage Fashion Model," the Barbie doll combined the popular fascination with high fashion and the new American emphasis on the "teenager." To Mattel, she was "an exciting, all-new kind of doll . . . shapely and grown up! . . . with fashion apparel authentic in every detail!" Although she was not the first fashion doll, Barbie would soon become far and away the most successful.

Mattel accurately predicted that "girls of all ages will thrill to the fascination of her miniature wardrobe of fine-fabric fashions: tiny zippers that really zip . . . coats with luxurious, carefully tailored linings . . . jeweled earrings, necklaces, and color-coordinated sunglasses!" The Basic Barbie Doll Fashion Model Set cost three dollars, and included an eleven-and-one-half-inch vinyl plastic doll, dressed in a black-and-white-striped jersey swimsuit, sunglasses, earrings, and high heels. Her twenty-one outfits could be purchased separately. "Moveable arms, legs, and head make it easy to dress Barbie in her exciting fashion model's wardrobe."

Barbie's early fashions were created by Charlotte Johnson, a free-lance fashion designer hired by Mattel. Like most American designers of the time, Johnson looked to the French haute couture for inspiration. Thus, Barbie's stylish wardrobe was closely modeled on contemporary high fashion, and every year new ensembles were launched. It took several years to develop the first collection; Barbie's "Gay Parisienne" (1959), a cocktail dress with a pouf skirt in pindot rayon taffeta, was based on a 1956 couture dress by Dior (page 26). This being the 1950s, Barbie's dress was completely accessorized, with color-coordinated high-heeled shoes, a veiled hat, long gloves, pearl necklace and earrings, a white fur stole, and a purse.

The couture quality of Barbie's fashions is immediately apparent in David Levinthal's beautiful photographs. One of my favorite images shows a brunette Barbie posed against a crimson background (page 18), wearing her Chanel-inspired navy-blue jersey suit, known to collectors as "Commuter Set" (1959). Like a real Chanel mannequin, Barbie is adorned with costume jewelry. The color of her red feather hat exactly matches her hatbox—and her lipstick. (The close-up photograph on page 51 also clearly shows her meticulous eye makeup and the extraordinary workmanship of the hat and beaded necklace.) Barbie's satin blouse is of better quality than most human-size blouses of today.

Like couture clothing, Barbie's fashions were exceptionally well made, with handsewn buttons, seams, and hems. They had real pockets and linings, and each garment had a label with the Barbie logo. The fabrics were designed and made to order for specific miniature fashions. Even the tiny zippers were specially made for the Barbie doll.

Who actually made Barbie's tiny clothes? Although Charlotte Johnson designed Barbie's wardrobe, the clothes themselves were produced in Japan. For economic reasons, Mattel had decided to work with a Japanese manufacturer, Kokusai Boeki

Kaishi Ltd., so in 1957 Johnson was brought to Tokyo, where she was assisted by a local seamstress, Fumiko Nakamura. Together, they developed a prototype of each fashion design. The prototype was then sent to a local factory, where sample makers reproduced it. These copies were sent to Mattel for approval, and approved samples were sent back to Japan for production. Most of the workers who cut and sewed the clothes were older Japanese women, although specialist subcontractors were responsible for accessories such as sunglasses.

Barbie's fashions had evocative names, such as "Red Flair" (1962), a gorgeous coat that was very similar to one worn by Jacqueline Kennedy (page 15). "On the Avenue" (1965), also known as "Sunday Visit," was a dramatic white-and-gold suit with a flyaway jacket, which looked as though it could have been designed by the great couturier Balenciaga (page 41). Fashion at this time was often intended for specific occasions, and many of Barbie's outfits bear names like "Saturday Matinee" (1965), a fur-trimmed tweed suit (page 24), or "Sorority Meeting" (1962), a cocoa brown sheath dress with matching knitted vest and pillbox hat (page 37).

Although her wardrobe was notable for formal attire, Barbie also had many clothes suitable for work, such as "Career Girl" (1963), a Balenciaga-inspired pepper-and-salt tweed suit (page 16), not dissimilar to Ken's "Business Appointment" (1966). Along with her many Paris-inspired fashions, her ensembles included casual American sportswear separates, as well as dramatic Italian styles.

During the 1950s, Italian fashions became popular with many Americans. A major article in *Life*, entitled "Italy Gets Dressed Up," reported rhapsodically on how Italy's "amazing postwar recovery" had resulted in the development of a "fledgling fashion industry" that attracted American buyers and was even said to "pose a challenge to Paris." The following year, in 1952, *Life* published another article, reporting that "Italy's fashions are becoming as well known as its table wine." Long recognized for its elegant accessories, Italy was now becoming known also for its luxurious sportswear.

Barbie's "Roman Holiday" (1959) evokes the casual elegance of Italian style (page 19). Like the movie of the same name, starring Audrey Hepburn, this ensemble has movie star glamour. Bold where Paris fashion was refined, "Roman Holiday" consisted of a red-and-white-striped coat over a sheath dress with matching top.

Naturally, the accessories were stylish. They included a red hat, a shiny white belt and matching purse, and sunglasses, as well as short white gloves, earrings, and, of course, high-heeled shoes. Like a number of the fashions photographed by Levinthal, "Roman Holiday" is today one of the rarest and most sought-after Barbie ensembles.

At the time, the most expensive of Barbie's ensembles was her wedding gown (page 43), which retailed for five dollars in 1960—compared with a simple day dress like "Cotton Casual" (1960), which cost only one dollar. Barbie's wedding dress was of flowered net with a high neck, long sleeves, and a long, full skirt lavishly overlaid with floral lace. The satin lining featured a romantic heart-shaped decolletage. Her wedding veil was held in place with a pearl band over her hair. She also wore a pearl necklace and earrings, and carried a bouquet of flowers. For good luck, she wore a blue garter. It was also possible, for twenty dollars, to buy an entire Trousseau Set, which included "everything for the wedding . . . and the honeymoon too."

Like the Mona Lisa, whose image has been liberated from the Louvre to enter popular culture, the Barbie doll is a familiar cultural icon. But although we thought we knew Barbie, Levinthal's photographs let us see her as if for the first time—as the quintessential fashion doll. Finally Barbie has a worthy fashion photographer! He succeeds in large part because he avoids the clichés that have developed around Barbie, while simultaneously acknowledging the wealth of information that her fans share.

"Solo in the Spotlight" (1960) was—and is—one of Barbie's most famous dresses. Back in 1994 Levinthal created a photograph, called *Barbie Noir*, which emphasized its dramatic intensity. In the photograph, Barbie stands slightly out of focus, like the memory of torch singers of the past, facing a sharply focused microphone. Unlike most of those who have photographed Barbie, Levinthal did so without the slightest element of kitsch, drawing attention instead to the almost magical power of Barbie's glamour. It was *Barbie Noir* which inspired the present *Barbie Series*, probably the most beautiful images of Barbie ever created.

For the *Barbie Series*, Levinthal worked with Laura Meisner, who dressed and posed the dolls. They chose to photograph "Solo in the Spotlight" without its usual accessories—no microphone, no pink scarf, no long black gloves, no beaded neck-lace. The photograph is cropped just above the ruffled hem adorned with a rose, effectively removing all anecdotal elements from the final picture, while emphasiz-ing the stark elegance of Barbie's most famous dress. Her glittering sheath thus bears an extraordinarily close resemblance to some of the most elegant couture evening dresses of the late 1950s. For the first time, we can see "Solo in the Spotlight" pri-marily in terms of its drop-dead chic (frontispiece).

Levinthal also photographed Barbie's famous pale pink evening dress, "Enchanted Evening" (1960) (page 70). But another, even more interesting picture simply alludes to it, with a dress form, swathed in pink satin, placed behind a crisply focused image of Barbie wearing "Busy Gal" (1960), a two-piece red linen suit with a red-and-white-striped blouse. "Busy Gal," in turn, alludes to Barbie's role as a fashion designer, for under her arm, she carries a portfolio of her fashion drawings (page 17). We can imagine that Barbie the fashion designer is in the process of cre-ating "Enchanted Evening," which she will later wear in her alternative role as fash-ion model.

In a particularly witty tableau, two Barbies are posed at an elegant lunch table (page 25). One of them wears the adorable pink suit "Fashion Luncheon" (1966), and the other wears a turquoise suit-dress called "Fashion Editor" (1965). In anoth-er photograph Barbie, wearing "Student Teacher" (1965), sits at a desk with her pointer and globe, not too secretly kicking off one of her red high-heeled pumps (page 66).

Barbie's multiplicity is evoked again in a photograph that shows a brunette Ponytail Barbie in a pink sweater set side by side with a blonde Ponytail Barbie in a blue and white sweater set (page 33). The brunette wears a skirt (ladylike) and gold hoop earrings (sexy); the blonde wears trousers (sporty) and pearl earrings (femi-nine), and has perched on her head a pair of sunglasses (for movie star glamour). They both have the sophisticated high-fashion face that characterized the original Barbie doll, with arched eyebrows, red lips, and side-glancing eyes.

Over the years, Barbie's facial expression, makeup, and hairstyle would evolve just as her clothing fashions did. In addition to her original ponytail, Barbie styled her hair in a side-part, flip, bubble cut, pageboy, and swirl. In 1963, Mattel even launched Fashion Queen Barbie with a wardrobe of wigs: "Now you can change her hair color and style as easily as you change her clothes." Soon there were Barbies with red hair and ash-blonde hair; there were light and dark brunettes, and also platinum blondes. When I was growing up, I had a blonde Barbie, but now I prefer the brunette pageboy. In the 1960s, though, the whole issue of hair was about to become much more controversial.

In 1964 the Beatles had their first hit, "I Want to Hold Your Hand." Suddenly, boys had long hair and girls had short skirts. London's Carnaby Street became world-famous for the latest mod fashions by designers like Mary Quant. In 1966 Mattel launched a new doll called Francie, who was described as Barbie's "MOD'ern cousin." As *Barbie* magazine explained: "*Mod* is short for modern and it means new. . . . *Cool* means anything that's great. . . . *Groovy* and *gear* are the same as cool. . . . So . . . if you're mod . . . that means you think Barbie and her friends are really *cool*." *Barbie* magazine also loved the Beatles: "Have you heard their latest song? Well, remember the first song they recorded . . . it's very different in melody, words and sound. That's what makes them so outstanding. Their style keeps on changing."

Soon Barbie's style would change, too. Because Francie was younger than Barbie she was the first to wear "new and swinging" styles like miniskirts, boots, and flares. Francie was quoted in *Barbie* magazine as saying: "I'm always trying something new! Here's what I dig the very most: Rock 'n roll dances (that's me doing the frug), loooooong hair (mine comes clear down to my shoulders), and wearing all the latest teenage styles!" But before you could say "Groovy!" Barbie had grown *her* hair long and adopted all the latest Youthquake fashions.

In her 1967 incarnation as Twist 'N Turn Barbie, she had bendable legs and could pivot at the waist. She had also acquired long straight hair and a brand-new face—younger, more wide-eyed, with long eyelashes. Mattel's first television commercial featuring the new doll showed a girl asking: "But what do I do with my old Barbie doll?" The answer was: Trade her in. In exchange for one old Barbie doll, plus one dollar and fifty cents, children could get a new Barbie, who looked younger and more innocent, sweeter and less sultry.

This transformation, of course, paralleled the shift in real fashion models away from the elegant, haughty goddesses of the 1950s, women like Dovima and Bettina, and towards girls like Jean Shrimpton and Twiggy. Barbie's couture period was over. In real life, too, Paris was increasingly eclipsed by the new styles coming out of Swinging London. When model Jean Shrimpton and fashion photographer David Bailey visited the New York offices of *Vogue*, editor Diana Vreeland called out, "The English have arrived!"

During Barbie's mod period, she adopted minidresses and flared trousers in wild colors like orange and hot pink, and in materials like vinyl and metallic knit. She put her hair in a long braid, and exchanged her stockings for lacy-patterned tights. By 1967, her fashions even showed the influence of Flower Power. Probably her most outstanding mod ensemble was "Intrigue" (1967), a metallic gold-painted polyester knit dress and trench coat (page 83). James Bond, move over! Wearing "Intrigue" made Barbie look like Emma Peel of *The Avengers* or the Girl from U.N.C.L.E.

Fashion is about change, and Barbie's fashions continued to evolve. Levinthal, however, has spared us the fashions of the 1970s, "the decade that taste forgot," and the 1980s (remember shoulder pads?). Although Barbie acquired some stylish designer fashions in the 1990s (I certainly wish I had the Donna Karan Barbie!), they are not shown here either, since contemporary fashion is simply too fragmented to be summed up in one doll's wardrobe. Barbie's dominant fashion statement today is pink and glittery, because that is what her child fans prefer. This, however, is a book about a time when fashion and Barbie were perfectly matched. With David Levinthal, Barbie finally has the fashion photographer she deserves.

VALERIE STEELE

Bubble Cut Barbie, 1962. "Red Flair" (1962–65).
Balenciaga was the inspiration for this red velvet coat,
which resembles one worn by Jacqueline Kennedy.

Dressed in similar pepper-and-salt tweed outfits, a Bubble Cut Barbie, 1962,
wearing Balenciaga-inspired "Career Girl" (1963–64), is shown with a bendable-leg Ken doll, 1965, sporting
"Business Appointment" (1966–67), and a Skipper doll, 1964, who wears "All Spruced Up!" (1967).

#3 Barbie, 1960. "Busy Gal" (1960–61). Barbie as fashion designer,
complete with portfolio, in a crisp red linen suit and striped blouse,
one of her many career-related ensembles.

17

#3 Barbie, 1960. "Commuter Set" (1959–60).
The Coco Chanel influence is apparent in this no-nonsense navy blue jersey
travel suit with a cardigan-style jacket and slim skirt.

#3 Barbie, 1960. "Roman Holiday" (1959).
This much-sought-after ensemble comes with a made-to-scale powder
compact (page 35), the rarest Barbie accessory.

Color Magic Barbie, 1966, wearing "Riding in the Park" (1966–67).

Color Magic Barbie, 1966. "Lunch on the Terrace" (1966).
Chartreuse plaid gingham is paired with multicolored dots to create a whimsical
yet elegant sheath dress and matching picture hat.

Bubble Cut Barbie, 1963. "Vacation Time" (1965), a pink rayon
bulky sweater and matching pink gingham shorts.

Bendable-leg Barbie, 1965. "Poodle Parade" (1965).
The accessories for this outfit include a dog-show trophy,
awarded to Barbie's winning poodle.

Bendable-leg Barbie, 1965. "Saturday Matinee" (1965).
This sensational gold-and-brown tweed suit and turban are reminiscent
of the glamorous forties.

Bendable-leg Barbies, 1966, in turquoise "Fashion Editor" (1965) and pink
"Fashion Luncheon" (1966), both outfits suitable for work.

Preceding pages: # 3 Barbie, 1960. "Gay Parisienne" (1959).
The playfully exaggerated silhouette of this blue-and-white pindot rayon taffeta
bubble dress pays tribute to Christian Dior.

Side-parted Bubble Cut Barbie, 1966. "Dinner at Eight" (1963).
Like many fashions of the period, this orange rayon and Mylar thread hostess
ensemble was designed for a specific occasion.

Ponytail Barbie, 1962. "In the Swim" (1964).
A blue Helanca maillot and a straw hat accented with a silk chiffon scarf.

Side-parted Bubble Cut Barbie, 1966. "Underfashions" (1966–67).
A pale pink tricot corselet and shimmering hose.

#6 Barbies, 1964. Pink "Knitting Pretty" (1964) and blue and white
"Mood for Music" (1962–63). These casual outfits feature
individually knitted sweater sets.

#4 Ponytail Barbies, 1960. A blonde and a brunette Barbie wear the same brocade cocktail sheath in gold (1959–62) and red (1963).

Accessories are a precious element of any vintage costume.
Shown here are the handbag for "Saturday Matinee" (1965), the "Roman
Holiday" compact (1959), and the Sears mink cape (1964).

Bubble Cut Barbie, 1965, in a black Helanca maillot (1962–63).

Side-parted Bubble Cut Barbie, 1966, models "Sorority Meeting" (1962–63),
a cocoa brown cotton sheath with a matching sleeveless knitted vest
and brown felt pillbox hat.

A Japanese side-parted American Girl Barbie, 1966, wearing a "Tuesday Taylor"
swimsuit (1969), is shown with a "Swirl" Ponytail Barbie, 1964, in a Helanca maillot
(1966) and a brunette Bubble Cut Barbie, 1962, sporting a spandex suit (1961).

Bubble Cut Barbie, 1962.

Bendable-leg Barbies, 1966. An oversize fur hat and a scarf-collared jacket that opens to reveal a
turquoise ruched silk chiffon bodice make "Gold 'N Glamour" (1965) a rare vintage ensemble.
It is shown here with "On the Avenue" (1965), a dramatic white-and-gold suit with a flyaway jacket.

Pages 43–45: #4 Barbie, 1960. "Wedding Day Set" (1959–62).

#6 Barbie, 1964. "Plantation Belle" (1959–61). This doll is particularly
desirable to collectors because of the lemon yellow shade of her blonde hair.

"Swirl" Ponytail Barbie, 1964. "Modern Art" (1965),
a flower-printed cotton overlaid with green silk georgette.

Bubble Cut and Ponytail Barbies, 1962, wearing "Dancing Doll" (1965)
and "Busy Morning" (1963).

"Magnificence" (1965), a splendid ball gown of red satin and pink silk chiffon.

#3 Barbie, 1960.

Bendable-leg Barbie, 1966. "Music Center Matinee" (1966–67).
This chic two-piece dress of red silk chiffon over silk taffeta is enhanced by an
extravagant shocking-pink picture hat.

Pages 55–57: Side-parted Bubble Cut Barbie, 1966. A sleek silk faille strapless
sheath, "Black Magic" (1964–65), captures the mystery of evening attire.

Bendable-leg Barbie, 1966. "Junior Prom" (1965).

Bubble Cut Barbie, 1963. "Sophisticated Lady" (1963–64). An unusually shaped
skirt heightens the style of this pink rayon gown decorated with silver lace. It
makes a regal ensemble when worn with its companion rose velvet coat (right).

Bendable-leg Barbie, 1966. "Matinee Fashion" (1965). Red linen, faux fur, and silk
chiffon make a striking combination in this sophisticated dinner suit.

Bubble Cut Barbie, 1961. "Red Silk Sheath" (1962–63).
Charlotte Johnson created a wardrobe of "real" clothes in miniature, such as this
simple yet bold dress for everyday.

Bendable-leg Barbie, 1966. "Student Teacher" (1965–66).

Bubble Cut Barbie, 1961. "Party Date" (1963), a cocktail dress of flocked
white satin speckled with gold glitter.

Pages 70, 72–73: Bubble Cut Barbie, 1963. "Enchanted Evening" (1960–63).
This famous pink taffeta strapless evening sheath with side drape is clearly a nod
to the couture designs of Charles James.

#3 Barbie, 1960. "Senior Prom" (1963–64), a bouffant gown of
blue and green satin overlaid with net, inspired by a design by Edith Head
for Elizabeth Taylor in the film *A Place in the Sun*.

Bendable-leg Barbie, 1967. "Gala Abend" (1967), the rarest and most
expensive of all vintage Barbie costumes, is shown on a strikingly beautiful
doll with pink skin tone and side-parted hair.

Bendable-leg Barbie, 1966.

Talking Barbie, 1970. "Silver Serenade" (1971–72).
Silver lamé opera gloves and a faux-fur boa accessorize a silver-and-turquoise
Lurex knit dress to create this fantastic evening ensemble.

Left: Twist 'N Turn Barbie, 1969. "Bermuda Holidays" (1967–68). This summer playsuit pairs up a color-saturated op-art flower-print tunic and hat with green Bermuda shorts. Above: Hair Fair Barbie, 1971. "Hot Togs" (1972). The orange hot pants and avocado green leggings are typical of mod period fashions. The Afghan came with this Alpine costume.

Talking Barbie, 1968. "Special Sparkle" (1970).
This pink-and-gold brocade coat and cinch belt are worn over a pink silk chiffon
blouse and gold lamé miniskirt (page 86).

Twist 'N Turn Barbie, 1967. "Glimmer Glamour" (1968).
A gold-knit coat opens to display a sparkling party dress of blue silk taffeta
overlaid with glittered silk chiffon.

Pages 83–85: Twist 'N Turn Barbie, 1969–71. "Intrigue" (1967–68). This cocktail
ensemble, a trench coat of brilliant gold-painted polyester knit worn over a matching
skirt and gold-and-white knit top, was influenced by the James Bond movies.

Twist 'N Turn Barbie, 1969. "Now Knit" (1970). The striped knit minidress,
clasped at the waist with a silver belt, is worn with an unusual but original
accessory, a lime green faux-fur hat.

Standard Barbie, 1967. "Sea Worthy" (1969). This turquoise and yellow
sailor dress is reminiscent of turn-of-the century children's clothing.

Above : Twist 'N Turn Barbies, 1967. Sold in Japan only, these suits have no names. Right : Twist 'N
Turn Barbies, 1967. "All That Jazz" (1968–69), an airy pleated dancing ensemble of striped silk organza in
pink, yellow, and gold, is shown with a red knit dress and coat manufactured exclusively for Japan.

ACKNOWLEDGMENTS

Most of the dolls reproduced in this book belong to Patrick McGovern, who gave unsparingly of his time and permitted us complete access to his extraordinary collection of mint vintage Barbie dolls and outfits. Doug James also lent us a doll from his collection; and Merle Davidson suggested other Barbie collectors who might participate in the project. Laura Meisner's love for dolls and keen understanding of them is evident in her meticulous styling of those photographed for the book. John Reuter of the Polaroid 20 x 24 Studio is responsible for the expert lighting of the pictures. Tricia Rosenkilde made 8 x 10 transparencies of the Polaroid 20 x 24 originals for reproduction, and provided assistance during the photographic process. Lisa Martin, David Levinthal's assistant, was an asset throughout the project; Christopher Ford of the Mark Moore Gallery was enthusiastically supportive. Katy Homans's elegant design enhances our appreciation of the images. Victoria Wilson of Alfred A. Knopf totally understood and wholeheartedly endorsed the book from its inception and made a valued contribution as editor, and her associate Lee Buttala graciously attended to endless details.

We are especially grateful to Cynthia Chace Wessling, whose initial support helped launch the book. Kathleen A. Meade was a continual resource; and Mary Ann Watts generously offered useful suggestions. Lastly, the enthusiasm and tireless efforts of Adrienne Fontanella and Mary Rafferty at Mattel were essential to the project.

Design and typesetting by Katy Homans

Separations by Elite Color Group, Providence, Rhode Island

Printed and bound by L.E.G.O. / Eurografica, Vicenza, Italy

Fashion Queen Barbie, 1963.
This silk crepe kimono was manufactured exclusively for the Japanese.